GREEK AND ROMAN TOPICS: 2

Sparta

Michelle Thompson

(1)

Susana Bustamante

SSB

1986/87.

GREEK AND ROMAN TOPICS

SPARTA

ROBIN BARROW
School of Education, University of Leicester

London
GEORGE ALLEN & UNWIN
Boston   Sydney

First published in 1975
Third impression 1983

GEORGE ALLEN & UNWIN LTD
40 Museum Street, London WC1A 1LU

© George Allen & Unwin (Publishers) Ltd 1975

ISBN 0 04 930002 4

For Roland

Printed in Great Britain
in 11 point Plantin
by Fletcher & Son Ltd, Norwich

CONTENTS

FURTHER STUDY

ACKNOWLEDGEMENTS

The author and publishers would like to express their thanks to Alan Donovan for the drawings he has contributed to this book, and to the following for permission to reproduce photographs: Museum of Sparta: 2a, 2b. Mr N. Georgiadis: 4, 8, 38. Athens National Archaeological Museum: 11, 14, 28, 33. British Museum: 13, 15, 21, 31. V. Karageorghis (Department of Antiquities, Nicosia): 16. Staatliche Museen, Berlin: 17. American School of Classical Studies at Athens: 20. Wadsworth Atheneum, Hartford, Connecticut: 18. Chatillon-sur-Seine Museum: 22. Professor F. Brommer (Archaeological Institute, University of Mainz): 23. Louvre (Photo, Chuzeville): 29. National Gallery: 32.

The story of Thermopylae

In 480 BC Xerxes, king of the enormous Persian empire, led an army of about 250,000 men to invade Greece. He was seeking revenge for the defeat the Greeks had inflicted on his father's troops ten years before, at the battle of Marathon. Xerxes did not intend to be defeated. He even went so far as to bridge the Hellespont with boats and to have a canal dug through Mount Athos, so that his soldiers could march down into Greece from the north and would not have to risk a voyage by sea.

He had at his court a Greek named Demaratus who had once been a king of Sparta. Xerxes wanted to know something about the enemy he was going to attack and so he naturally turned to Demaratus.

'Which of the Greeks,' he asked, 'will dare to resist me? It seems to me that even if all the Greeks joined together and were helped by other people as well, they would stand no chance against my army.'

'I have a very high opinion of most of the Greeks,' replied

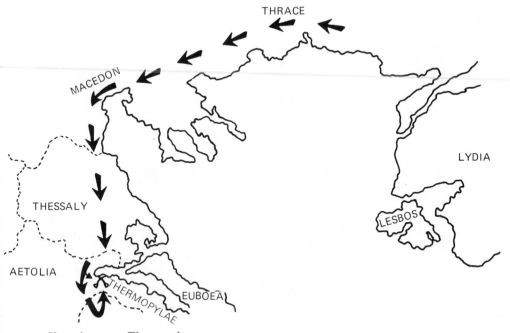

1 *Xerxes' route to Thermopylae.*

Demaratus, 'but I am only talking about the Spartans now. Under no circumstances will *they* make peace with you on terms that involve the surrender of Greece to Persia. They will fight, even if all the other Greeks give in. And do not ask me whether they have enough men to fight you. If only a thousand of them march out to battle, then that thousand will fight you.'

Xerxes laughed. 'Do you really think that a thousand men, of whatever sort, would dare to fight an army the size of mine? Besides, the Spartans are not even compelled to fight as my soldiers are. They are free to do as they please. Do you really imagine that so few would freely choose to fight?'

'I have already told you that they will,' replied Demaratus. 'In single combat the Spartans are as good as any soldiers on earth. Fighting together they are the best in the world. You are right: they are free in a sense. But they do have a master – the law. Whatever the law demands, they do. And the law always demands the same thing: never retreat in battle, whatever the odds. Always stand your ground. Win or die.' (Herodotus, *The Histories*, 7.101.)

When Xerxes' army reached Thermopylae, a narrow pass through which it had to go, the way was blocked by a few thousand Greeks led by Leonidas and 300 Spartans. The Greeks might have held the pass for a very long time since the superior numbers of the Persians were no help to them in such a confined space. But the Greeks were

2a and b *Leonidas.*

betrayed. Somebody led the Persians round to the back of the pass by another route. Quickly Leonidas sent most of the Greek soldiers back, but he and his 300 Spartans, with a few others, stood their ground against the onrush of Persians from in front and behind. They knew their task was hopeless. They could not hope to win. They chose to die.

They were killed to the last man and buried where they fell. Over their graves was written: 'Stranger, go and tell the Spartans at home that we lie here in obedience to the law.'

The story of Leonidas and the Three Hundred is only one of many stories about the Spartans that show how important courage and obedience were to them. They were a people who preferred death to dishonour, and military glory to everything else. They were a small community of warriors who took little interest in material comfort, riches or beautiful works of art. Complete loyalty to the state was demanded of every Spartan. They had virtually no freedom to do anything of which the city as a whole did not approve.

If you look at the pictures of what remains of Sparta, you may find it difficult to believe that it was ever a very important place. All that is left is a single pillar on top of a small hill and a pile of uninteresting-looking stones beside the hill. In comparison, the remains of a city like Athens look magnificent and make it clear that

3 *Remains of the Spartan Acropolis. These remains date from a later period in Sparta's history.*

4 *The theatre at Sparta. These remains also belong to a later period.*

Athens must once have been a great and important city. But Sparta was also once famous and powerful. For 300 years (700 BC–400 BC) she was in fact one of the most powerful of all the Greek cities. And at one point, at the end of the long Peloponnesian war (431–404), she and her allies actually crushed Athens and the mighty Athenian empire, and then, for a brief time, Sparta was the unchallenged master of the Greek world.

This is the only book in the present series which is not about both the Greeks and the Romans. The reason for this is that there were no other people quite like the Spartans either in the rest of Greece or in the Roman world. They organised their life in their own particular way, had their own customs, their own problems and their own view of what was important. They seemed peculiar even to the other Greeks, and to us, as we find out more about them, they will probably seem even more so.

5 *The entrance to the Athenian Acropolis.*

6 *The Parthenon.*

Thessaly

Thermopylae
Doris
Locris
Phocis
Euboea
●Delphi
Boeotia
●Thebes

Achaia
Attica ╳Marathon
Megaris
●Megara
Corinth
●Athens

Elis
Arcadia
Argolis

Messenia
Laconia
Taygetus Mountains
●Sparta
Pylos●

0   25   50 miles
0   40   80 km

Cythera

7 *The Peloponnese.*

CHAPTER ONE

The Emergence of Sparta

Sparta

The name 'Sparta' is sometimes loosely used to refer to the whole of the southern half of the Peloponnese (that is, the whole peninsula of southern Greece). And the name 'Spartans' is sometimes used to refer to all the people who lived in this area. This is because the whole area, which contains Laconia and Messenia, was ruled by the Spartans. But strictly speaking, the name Sparta refers only to the city situated by the river Eurotas, which flows through Laconia, and the Spartans were the people who belonged to that city. It was also known as Lacedaemon.

Sparta was not built around a high and defensible hill or citadel, as most Greek cities were; and the Spartans never built walls around their city, as did the Athenians, for example. In fact the city of Sparta was not originally one community at all, but was made up of five separate villages which lay close together. The reason why the Spartans never troubled to build defensive walls must originally have been that they relied instead upon the natural defences of the surrounding land. For although the city itself is in the river valley, where crops could be raised successfully on the plains, between the valley and the rest of Greece is a line of high and rocky mountains. Any enemy would have had difficulty in crossing these, and the Spartans could have defended them relatively easily. Besides, the Spartans had a reputation for being the best of all Greek foot soldiers, and this deterred enemies from travelling on a long and difficult journey to challenge them to battle.

The Spartans, then, were less worried than the inhabitants of most Greek cities about enemies from outside their territory. But they were very concerned indeed about an enemy *within* their own territory. This enemy was the enormous slave population of serfs or *helots* as they were called. Defensive walls around the city would not have helped them against this enemy, for their problem was not how to defend themselves against the *helots*, but how to keep the

8 *A mountain range beyond Sparta.*

helots enslaved. It would have been no use hiding behind city walls. The Spartans had to control the *helots* throughout Laconia and Messenia. They had to prevent them from ever getting the chance to band together and rise in armed rebellion.

We shall now see how this situation first arose.

The Dark Ages

The Spartans were a different race of people from most of the *helots* and possibly from some of the other inhabitants of Laconia. They were also different from many other Greeks, including the Athenians. The Athenians were Ionians, and the Ionians were one of the earliest peoples to live in Greece. But the Spartans were Dorians who had come to Greece long after the Ionians.

In about 1000 BC the Dorians, a wandering and relatively un-

9 *This diagram illustrates the defensive walls that were built around Athens and her harbours. Note how they virtually transform Athens into an island.*

1. *City of Athens*
2. *Phaleron wall*
3. *Phaleron bay*
4. *Piraeus*

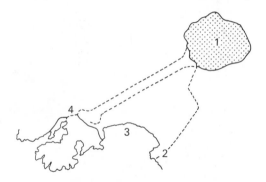

civilised people, invaded Greece from the north. They probably did not arrive in one group like a conquering army, but came in separate bands over a period of years. We do not really know a great deal about this invasion because the Dorians, being a primitive people compared with those already settled in Greece, could not write, and therefore left no written records of what went on. Furthermore, they destroyed all that was left of the earlier civilisation.

The next 200 years are known to historians as the Dark Ages for two reasons. First, because they *are* dark to us: we know virtually nothing about them. And second, because the little we do know makes

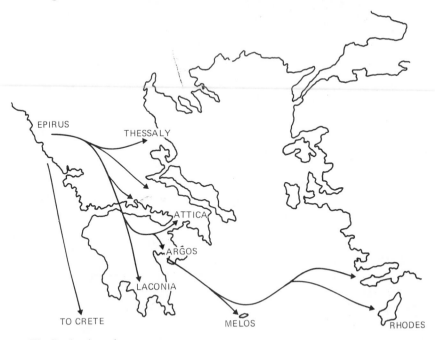

10 *The Dorian invasion.*

11 *Early Greek jewellery.*
Seventh century BC.

LYDIA

CHIOS

ATTICA

SAMOS

12 *The Ionian migration.*

it clear that it was an uncivilised and backward time. The Dorian invaders were like savages compared with the people they overran. Cities were destroyed or deserted; the art of writing, which had gradually come into use in some parts of Greece by this time, was lost. The beauty and skill that the earlier Greeks had put into the making of armour, jewellery, pottery and building, disappeared completely for a time.

Most of the earlier inhabitants retreated eastwards, some to places such as Athens, others overseas to what is now Asia, but then became known as Ionia. Meanwhile, the Dorians proceeded down into the Peloponnese where for the most part they settled. But first they had to deal with the remains of the original population, and these were the people whom they defeated and enslaved – the people who became the *helots*.

At the beginning of the Dark Ages there must have been a number of Dorian settlements in Laconia, each independent but friendly towards the others, and each controlling its own *helot* population. But at some later date the Spartans gained the upper hand over the neighbouring Dorian communities and took control of the whole of Laconia and all the *helots*. They did not enslave their fellow Dorians. Instead they allowed them a certain amount of freedom provided that they obeyed whatever orders the Spartans chose to give. These people became known as *perioeci*, which means simply 'those who live round about'.

Finally, the Spartans turned on the people of neighbouring Messenia. It is not clear whether these people were Dorians like themselves or the unconquered descendants of the original inhabitants. Whichever they were, there is no doubt about what happened to them. By about 700 BC, after a long and bloody series of battles, the Messenians were enslaved as *helots*.

And so within about 300 years of the Dorian invasion, one small group, the Spartans, had become masters of half the Peloponnese. Most of the original population were now ruthlessly enslaved to them as *helots*, and their fellow Dorians, though not enslaved, had become their subjects, the *perioeci*.

Sparta after the Dark Ages

Gradually Greece emerged from the Dark Ages. Men began to discover again what had been lost; the destruction was over and cities began to develop again out of the ruins. Settlers were sent out to colonise new lands. Cities began to trade, not only within Greece, but abroad as well. New techniques were developed for making pottery, and painters experimented with new designs on vases. Skill and care were once again applied to such things as metal and woodwork; attention was once again devoted to sculpture and building. The art of writing was rediscovered, and the arts of poetry and music began to develop. It was an age of experiment and excitement.

To begin with, Sparta played her part in all this. To begin with, there was nothing particularly remarkable about her, except the extent of her power and the fact that she was in control of the *helots*. Poets and musicians lived in Sparta, including some of the most famous, such as Tyrtaeus and Terpander, who was said to have invented a seven-stringed lyre in place of the normal four-stringed type. Temples were built which we have no reason to suppose were

13 *An Athenian vase (c. 540 BC) showing Achilles fighting the Amazon Queen.*

14 *Clay head of a warrior.
About 700 BC.*

15 *A Spartan cup. Late sixth century BC.*

inferior in any way to other early Greek temples. Spartan pottery was decorated as carefully and well as that of any other city at the time, and Sparta was as advanced as any of her neighbours in other fields such as metal and woodwork. She had ships with which she traded with other parts of the Greek world. She was particularly famous for the choral dances that her citizens performed in honour of the gods, for her hospitality to strangers, and for the high standard of athletics amongst her citizens. Athletics were always an important feature of life for the Greeks, and there were more champions recorded from Sparta at the Olympic games during the early years of that festival than from any other city.

And then there was a change. From about the middle of the sixth century at the latest, the Spartans began to turn their backs on the rest of Greece. Far from welcoming visitors, they now kept foreigners out of their territory. They cut their trading activities considerably and ceased to build ships. When other cities began to use coinage, Sparta continued to use the traditional awkward iron bars as money. Of course the Spartans still had poetry and music, but they clung to the compositions of the past; new poets, new musicians with new ideas were not welcome. They still produced pottery, metalwork and woodwork – they needed to for everyday use – but Spartan productions were of poorer quality than the work of most other cities. Athletic exercise was still extremely important, but Spartans no

16 *Iron spits, used as money by the Spartans.*

17 *A Spartan cup showing warriors returning home with their dead.*

longer left Laconia to compete at festivals in other parts of Greece. We hear of no more Spartan competitors at Olympia, for instance.

While the rest of Greece was filled with a spirit of adventure and an enthusiasm for progress and change, Sparta retreated into the past. She no longer communicated with the rest of Greece, but became secretive and withdrawn. It was as if another Dark Age was beginning, but this time it applied only to the Lacedaemonians.

It is with the way of life that had now emerged that we are concerned in this book.

CHAPTER TWO

The Spartans

A Spartan king, Agesilaus, was once in command of a military expedition that included some of Sparta's allies. He ordered all the allies, regardless of what city they came from, to sit on one side of him and all the Spartans on the other. A herald was then told to announce that anybody who was a potter by trade, on either side, should stand up. After that all blacksmiths on either side were ordered to do the same. Next all masons were told to stand, then all carpenters, and so on, through all the various trades. By this time virtually all the allied soldiers were standing up. But not a single Spartan had stood. Then Agesilaus laughed and said: 'You see, my friends, how many *soldiers* we send out compared to you.'

The point was that the Spartans were full-time professional soldiers. From an early age they were trained to fight and drilled in battle tactics; this training continued throughout their adult life. A battle-line of Spartans was a line of soldiers who were physically fit, obedient to command, courageous and skilled. And as well as being professional soldiers they looked it: once a Spartan boy had reached manhood he was allowed to let his hair grow long, although up to that time he had to have it very short. This long hair was supposed to make the warriors look taller and more terrifying to the enemy. Before they joined battle the Spartans curled their hair neatly, put on red cloaks, and then took up their bronze shields. Their swords were short, but, as one of them once

18 *Bronze statuette of a Spartan warrior.*

said, they were long enough to reach their enemies.

Other Greek cities formed their armies only when a battle was about to take place. They simply called on their citizens to leave their farms or whatever trade they practised and to take up arms for the duration of a campaign. But the Spartans were not allowed to be shoemakers or carpenters; they were not allowed to have any kind of trade at all. To have a trade, to be involved in manufacturing something, was regarded as a low occupation and quite beneath the dignity of Spartans.

The distribution of land in Sparta

In a similar way, aristocrats in Victorian England used to look down on those who made their living in business. But Victorian aristocrats did not object to looking after their estates and their farming interests. The Spartans did not even regard superintending their land as worthy of their personal attention; instead a system was devised whereby the Spartans could be sure of having their food provided without actually having to trouble themselves about the farming.

A great deal of land in Laconia and Messenia was owned by the state, that is to say by the city of Sparta. This land was divided into thousands of equal estates, which were distributed equally amongst the Spartans. The rest of the land was privately owned, either by Spartans in addition to their estate, or by *perioeci*. But the state-owned land was the best, and each estate produced sufficient food for a Spartan and his family. Every Spartan was granted the right to his estate at birth, and when he died it went back to the state.

It was the *helots*, however, who were left with the responsibility of farming these estates. They cultivated the land, grew and collected the crops. The Spartans had no interest in the land, provided that the *helots* produced their food. The amount that had to be handed over was fixed by law, and anything that was left over the *helots* were allowed to keep for themselves. In a good year for crops the *helots* would no doubt have ample to eat, but in a bad year it was they who suffered.

The Equals

The Spartans, then, uninterested in trade and with their food provided, could devote their whole attention to the task of being soldiers. They were known as the *homoioi*, which means the 'Equals'. They may originally have been called the Equals because of the common life they shared, and the equal wealth and estates they were supposed to have. If this is so, the name gradually became less appropriate, because towards the end of the period we are concerned

19 *Spartan warriors in battle.*

with, some families had become richer than others, obviously as a result of acquiring more of the private land. But the name 'Equals' was probably also intended to signify that the Spartan soldier did not live and fight for himself alone. Everything he did was done equally for Sparta, or, to put it another way, for his Spartan comrades. Like the three musketeers, the Spartans were one for all and all for one.

To be a Spartan Equal, it was not enough simply to be a good soldier. In the first place, one had to be the son of a mother and father who were both Spartan. Secondly, one had to be brought up in the strict discipline of a Spartan education (which we shall look at more closely in Chapter Five). Thirdly, one had to belong to a dining or mess club, which was called a *syssition*.

The syssitia

These *syssitia* consisted of groups of fifteen people who always ate their dinner together. At the age of twenty a Spartan was eligible to join such a club, but he had to be accepted by all the members. They voted by dropping pellets of bread into a bowl; if the vote was in favour of the young man's election, the pellet was rolled into a ball; if it was against, it was squashed flat. Once elected to a *syssition*, the

20 *The shield of a Spartan captured at Pylos.*

Spartan had to provide a share of food from his estate equal to that supplied by his companions. He also had to attend every evening for the rest of his life, unless he was actually ill or away hunting or attending a public sacrifice. These *syssitia* must have contributed greatly to maintaining the feeling that the comradeship of the Equals was more important than a man's family or his private life.

The code of honour of the Spartan Equals

Finally, the Equals had a code of behaviour to which they clung rigidly. To remain an Equal it was necessary to keep to that code of behaviour, and the most important point in it was that cowardice should never be shown. If any Spartan did display cowardice in battle a special decree was passed, publicly disgracing him. And it was not only things like running away that counted as cowardice. There was one occasion on which 120 Spartans were trapped on an island near Pylos and captured by the Athenians. The prisoners were returned when peace was made, and the Spartans wanted to pass a decree of disgrace against the 120, because they had allowed themselves to be captured alive. The only reason why the decree was not passed was that the population was so low at that date (424 BC) that the Spartans could not afford to expel so many from the Equals.

If a man was disgraced, not only did he lose his political rights, but he was also made to wear special clothes and walk about unshaven, so that everybody would recognise him for a coward. No one would eat with him; no one would take exercise with him; no one would marry him, or his daughters. At public gatherings he had to sit alone.

There seem to have been a number of people in Laconia who were not full Spartans or *perioeci* or *helots*. Some of these may have been the children of Spartan fathers and *helot* mothers, and a few may have been *helots* who had been granted their freedom. But some of them must certainly have been Spartan Equals who had been disgraced.

Size of the Spartan population

Although they had to control all Messenia and Laconia, and rule over the *perioeci* and *helots*, the Spartans themselves were very few in number. Athens, one of the largest Greek cities, had about 50,000 male citizens. There were possibly as many as 10,000 Spartans in about 700 BC, but towards the end of the fifth century BC the number had dwindled to something nearer 1,000. This is remarkable, for although we do not know the exact numbers of either the *perioeci* or the *helots*, it is certain that each group must have outnumbered the Spartans by several thousand. If the *perioeci* and *helots* had ever joined together in an attempt to rebel, it is unlikely that the Spartans, trained soldiers though they were, would have been able to keep them in check. The *helots* did try on their own more than once, but the *perioeci* never joined with them, and so the Spartans were able to hold down the attempted rebellions. In the next chapter we shall see why the *perioeci* were prepared to accept the leadership of the Spartans.

21 *A Spartan warrior wearing his military cloak.*

CHAPTER THREE

The Perioeci

The *perioeci* lived in small villages or towns scattered around Laconia. They were extremely important for the maintenance of the Spartan system, partly because of the work they did and partly because they never chose to join forces with the *helots*.

The Spartans left them with considerable freedom. Each town was allowed to govern itself as it chose, provided, of course, that it did not try to break away from Sparta or interfere with Spartan policy. It was only in decisions about war or foreign policy generally that the *perioeci* had no independence at all. Whenever the Spartans went into battle, the *perioeci* were called out and expected to fight alongside them.

22 *The Vix crater.*

Trade and manufacture

But the *perioeci* were not brought up and trained as soldiers like the Spartans. They had quite a different function to perform. It was they who provided all the craftsmen, tradesmen and manufacturers in Laconia, since the Spartans were forbidden to practise these activities. Clothing, shoes, furniture and so on were all made by *perioeci* and then sold to the Spartans. The few examples of drinking-cups, statuettes and pottery that have been discovered at Sparta by archaeologists must have been the work of *perioeci*.

It was the Spartans who originally began to regard luxury and beauty as unnecessary, and comfort and decoration as unsuited to a warrior class. But this preference for the simple and useful gradually spread throughout Laconia. The *perioeci* became used to simple products themselves, as a result of having to produce austere goods for the Spartans. Their furniture was made of wood and no examples have survived; but the examples of their pottery and metal work that we have, dating from the period after 600 BC, are plainer and less skilfully produced than most of those found in other parts of Greece.

The *perioeci* had land adjoining their towns which they were free to work as they wished. But only a few of them were farmers, and these were the poorer ones, since their land consisted of whatever was left over after the Spartans had taken the best for their estates. The Spartans had no wish to encourage the *perioeci* to take up farming, because the carefully planned system that gave each of the three groups of people in Laconia a special job to do required the *perioeci* to be the craftsmen.

Why the perioeci did not rebel

We cannot be sure why the *perioeci* accepted their subordinate position. Perhaps they felt that on their own they could not achieve much against Spartan soldiers and that the *helots* were too inferior and contemptible to be their allies. (There may have been some racialist feeling in this, since the *perioeci* were Dorians and the *helots* were not.) But it is possible that they were really quite contented and saw little to complain about. They had security as members of a powerful and stable state; the system gave them an important job to do; and for the most part they were free to do as they wanted. The only real limitation on their freedom was their duty to fight when called upon to do so, and even this may not have been as objectionable to them as it may seem to us.

In the first place, all Greeks were fairly often engaged in fighting of some sort during these centuries. War was something that just happened and nobody made any real effort to establish lasting peace. In the second place, despite the fact that war was regarded as natural by the Greeks, there is one important point about the Spartans that we have not yet mentioned: although they were a warrior class, they had a reputation for being slow to go to war. Of course they sometimes did, but on the whole it seems that their army was not designed for foreign conquest. So the *perioeci* were not in fact obliged to fight any more than they would have been as citizens of many other cities. And if the fact that the Spartans could summon them to battle was no particular hardship, they may well have regarded themselves as quite lucky people, left to enjoy a peaceful and relatively secure life.

But if the Spartan state was not organised like a military camp in order to conquer the Greek world, why was it organised in this particular way? Part of the answer is certainly that the system was designed to keep the *helots* in slavery.

23 *Handle of an early bronze waterpot.*

CHAPTER FOUR

The Helots

Once their military way of life had been in existence for a few generations, the Spartans looked upon it as something greatly to be admired. But, almost certainly, the system had originally arisen in order to meet the threat of a revolt by the *helots*. The most likely time for the changes in Sparta to have occurred is at the end of the wars the Spartans fought against Messenia. When they had finally won those wars, they suddenly found themselves with twice the area of land to control and twice the number of *helots* to keep in check. They must then have realised that they could only survive if they became permanent professional soldiers. Although they later came to take pride in their military life for its own sake, they could never afford to ignore the possibility of a *helot* revolt. In fact, on more than one occasion, various groups of *helots* did try to rebel. But the Spartans were able to crush them. And they were able to prevent any wider revolt by all the *helots* because of the careful and sometimes brutal way in which they controlled them. The *helots* seldom had the opportunity even to consider fighting back. Virtually all the laws and all the arrangements in Sparta and throughout the Spartans' territory were designed with the purpose of keeping the *helots* in slavery.

Treatment of helots

Almost unbelievable stories are told about the harsh and humiliating way in which the *helots* were treated. According to one historian, the Spartans used to make some of the *helots* drunk so that they would behave in a particularly ludicrous and embarrassing manner; they deliberately made the *helots* make fools of themselves in this way, so that Spartan children would be warned against drinking too much. The *helots* were also made to play the buffoon by performing absurd dances and singing silly songs. Another ancient author tells us that each year a certain number of *helots* were selected for a public beating, just to encourage the rest to behave properly and cause no trouble. It is even said that any *helot* who seemed particularly strong and healthy was killed, for fear that he might lead a rebellion. There was also an organisation rather like a secret police system, which was known as the *Crypteia*. Apparently the purpose of the *Crypteia* was simply to keep the *helots* in a state of fear and subjection; from time to time young Spartans were armed with daggers and told to roam about the countryside at night, murdering any *helots* they could find.

It is very difficult to be certain how true these stories are. There certainly was a *Crypteia*, but perhaps the young men were only sent out to murder particular *helots* who the Spartans suspected might attempt to lead a revolt. Some of the other stories, too, may be exaggerated. But we do know that at the beginning of each year the newly elected magistrates made a formal declaration of war on the *helots*, which indicates that they regarded them as permanent enemies of the state, whom they would be quite prepared to kill if they were in any way a threat. We know, too, of one particular occasion on which the Spartans announced that the *helots* should themselves pick out those of their number who had done most service for their state in battle. (For surprising as it may seem, in view of the risk involved to the Spartans, *helots* were sometimes given arms and expected to fight during foreign wars.) Naturally the *helots* assumed that those selected would be rewarded in some way. But in fact the Spartans had realised that those who were selected would be the strongest and most courageous, and therefore the most dangerous to them. About 2,000 were chosen, and were led off in a triumphant procession with garlands on their heads as a mark of honour. They probably thought they were about to be granted their freedom. They were never heard of again. They were secretly killed.

It is not surprising that the Spartans were always concerned about the possibility of a revolt and that they used these harsh measures to keep the *helots* in suppression. It was not only that the *helots* far outnumbered them; the *helots* also represented a particular threat to the Spartans because, unlike the slave population of most Greek cities, they belonged to the land in which they were enslaved, and were all members of the same race. They were therefore much more likely to join together in an attempted rebellion than the slaves at Athens, for instance, who came from different parts of the world and spoke different languages.

What the helots *had to do*
There was a slightly brighter side to the *helots'* life. As we have seen, most of them were left to work on the land and that is not the most unpleasant of tasks. (A few may have been used as house slaves.)

They were allowed to live on their own, with their families, which was not always the case with slaves at Athens. And they were not dependent on the goodwill of an individual master, for they were not owned by private individuals, but by the city of Sparta as a whole. The city distributed them to individuals who then had

24 *An early plough (drawing of a figurine).*

a limited responsibility for them and some degree of control over them. But they did not have the power to do what they liked with the *helots* who were allotted to them to work their estates; they did not have any power of life or death over them. Only the state could authorise the killing of a *helot*. Apart from farming, the usual duties of a *helot* would include serving as a batman or military servant to a Spartan warrior when he was on campaign. And very occasionally *helots* were actually given their freedom.

But the fact remains that the *helots* were ruthlessly controlled by the Spartans. They were essential to the Spartan system, since the warrior class of Equals could only pursue their military way of life if they could be sure that everyday necessities such as food would be provided for them. Without the *helots* their way of life would have been impossible.

CHAPTER FIVE

Spartan Education

One ancient writer says that the Spartans did not 'approve of children learning music, writing and reading'. Another, an Athenian, who was probably just being rude, says that they were quite illiterate. And yet a third report claims that most of them could not count. None of these statements can be entirely true, but it is quite clear that the Spartan idea of education was very different from that of other Greeks and certainly from ours. Children were probably taught to form letters so that they could read simple messages, and to count to some extent. But the Spartans were not interested in literature and what we would call intellectual or academic activities. They did not study subjects like maths or science, geography or history. Nor were they concerned to teach their children to think for themselves or to acquire knowledge. They were suspicious of discussions about such things as science, other countries, the gods or how people ought to live. The Spartans saw no need for such discussions, because they did not intend to change their way of life or their beliefs, and they did not want any of their children to grow up with different ideas. As far as they were concerned, Sparta had perfected city life and the Equals were the best sort of people one could ask for. All that mattered was to bring up the next generation of children in such a way that they would be obedient to the state and would have the courage and strength required of a warrior.

The first stage of a Spartan boy's education
Very young children were brought up by nurses, not by their mothers. The nurses did not spoil the children in their care. Spartan children were brought up to eat whatever simple food was put before them and to become used to being left alone or left in the dark. We are told that they did not cry or sulk. Presumably, since most children cannot help crying or being in a bad temper at times, this means that nobody

took any notice of them or tried to comfort them when they did cry or sulk.

At the age of seven all boys were removed from their homes, and from that time until they were thirty years old they lived entirely in communal barracks. (You can read about the way in which Spartan girls were brought up in the next chapter.) In their barracks the boys were split into companies, and the companies were divided into platoons. The city appointed a *paidonomos* or warden who had absolute authority over the boys and who had the right to punish them if they misbehaved. To help him in this task he was accompanied by a group of young men over the age of eighteen (*eirens*) who carried whips with them. Their job, however, was only to correct those who behaved badly in some way. In the normal course of events the day-to-day activities of the platoons were organised by prefects or platoon captains. These were older boys, selected because they had shown good conduct and particular courage throughout their own early education. They had the right to give orders and to administer punishment to anyone who disobeyed them.

The object of this first stage of education was very simple: to develop the physical strength of the children and to teach them to live together and to show obedience. So instead of having lessons as we would understand them, young Spartan children went through an experience that was something like living all the year in a boy scout camp. They learnt how to look after themselves, how to get on with other people, how to respond promptly to orders and how to share responsibilities. Apart from these 'lessons' in living the Spartan way, the only other important part of this early education was physical exercise and training in athletics. Wearing only light tunics, with no shoes and with their hair close shaven, the 7- and 8-year-olds

25 *Spartan youths wrestling.*

were put through the first paces of a training designed to turn them into Spartan heroes.

The second stage of the Spartan boy's education

When the boys reached the age of twelve their education became even more disciplined and harsh. Even in winter time they were only allowed to wear one garment. This was probably a rough tunic, thicker than the one generally worn in summer; but winters in Greece are very cold, and it would not have been much help in keeping warm. They had to sleep on beds made out of rushes which they picked themselves from the river edge. (Rushes are not very comfortable to lie on and it is difficult to pick them without cutting one's hands. But as a result of having to do this continually the boys developed tough skins.) They were given very little food, for two reasons: in the first place it was believed that a small and simple diet tended to produce taller and healthier people. But secondly, and more important, the fact that they were provided with such limited rations more or less forced the children to rely on themselves to obtain more food. They learnt to live off the land, even stealing from the estates throughout the country. This was regarded as a valuable lesson in learning to look after oneself and not having to depend on other people. However, if a boy was caught stealing he was punished with a whipping and then, in addition, given even smaller rations.

Music and dance

A great deal of this secondary stage of education consisted of taking part in various contests and competitions. Obviously athletic competitions and games were very important; but there were also musical competitions.

Even though the Spartans had lost interest in experimenting and developing new tastes and fashions in their poetry and music, they still valued the old songs and the works of the poets and musicians of the past. They particularly liked the work of patriotic poets such as Tyrtaeus, who praised the city as being more important than the individual, as we can see from this poem:

A man who only has skill at wrestling is nothing to me.
Nor do I admire a man just because he can run faster than the wind.
Let a man be handsome, let him be rich—
Still I would not be impressed.
Courage, and courage alone, I respect.
For a man is useless in war
Unless he can bear to gaze on blood and slaughter unflinchingly

And take the enemy face to face.
This is courage. This is man's greatest virtue.
This is the most glorious prize that a young man can win.
And if he should die in the great struggle—
Why, then all will grieve for him.
The whole city will mourn him.
His memory will live for ever.
Though dead, he is immortal.

There was no real distinction between music, poetry and song in the Greek world. Poetry was generally recited to the accompaniment of a flute or lyre. The flute was particularly suitable for marching songs, such as the poem by Tyrtaeus, and the lyre for poetry that could be danced to or sung by choirs. Spartan boys therefore were taught to play the lyre and flute as well as learning the poetry that had long been honoured in the city. They also learnt the traditional dances.

Not surprisingly, in both their musical and athletic competitions, the Spartans favoured team games or contests, for they did not like to encourage the idea of individuals competing and showing themselves superior to others. The society of Equals had no place for individual champions or experts, and so children were brought up

26 *A lyre-player.*

27 *A flute-player.*

to take pride in the success of a group, of which each one was merely a small part, rather than in their own private successes. Rival teams competed in athletic contests and games; rival choirs sang in musical competitions, and rival groups of dancers competed against each other. The individual did not matter at Sparta. What mattered was the group, the platoon, the city.

28 *A ball game.*

Supervision

Even when they went out for a walk Spartan children had to obey rules: they had to walk in silence, with their hands under their cloaks and their eyes cast down to the ground. They were kept continually busy. And they were constantly watched over and observed by adults.

When they practised their dances or wrestling in the *palaestra* (an open-air sandy exercise area), or when they went through their military drill, their performance was judged and they were given advice and encouragement or criticism by anyone who happened to be present.

But adult supervision went further than this. Any citizen had the right to give an order to any child at any time, and also the right to punish him for failure or disobedience. Adults often deliberately tried to stir up arguments or quarrels between the children in order to see how they reacted. They were anxious to know which children would attempt to avoid a fight, and which would show courage and spirit. There was virtually no time of the day when somebody – a prefect, the *paidonomos*, some adult – was not watching over the children and ready to remind them of their duty, or to punish them if they failed to do it.

The third stage of a Spartan boy's education

The final stage of education began at the age of nineteen. The boy was now an *eiren* and could himself become a prefect of one of the platoons. He did not become a fully qualified soldier until the age of twenty-four, and he did not become a fully qualified citizen until the age of thirty. But at the age of nineteen he was technically an adult and could be called upon to fight if necessary.

By this time, of course, the young men had learnt all that the Spartans expected them to learn. It was just a question of continuing to keep fit and strong, continuing to show obedience and loyalty to the city, and getting further practice in the skills necessary for a soldier. Nevertheless, this stage provided some of the toughest activities that a Spartan had to take part in. For example, a primitive kind of rugby was played in which two sides of about fifteen people simply fought each other to get and keep possession of the ball, and in this fight any kind of wrestling technique was allowed. Then once every year there was a staged fight involving all the young men. It took place on a flat piece of ground surrounded by water and the fighting was brutal: they kicked, bit and gouged each other, as each side tried to drive the other into the water.

As if this sort of thing was not enough to keep the Spartans tough and on their mettle, during the course of each year the magistrates picked out three of the most promising young men and ordered each of them to pick a hundred more. The three chose those of their friends whom they most admired, and they had to state publicly why they admired them. This business of selection naturally caused resentment on the part of those who were not chosen by any of the three. That was the whole idea, for the result was that the 300 chosen were constantly on the look-out for opportunities to prove themselves superior to those not chosen, while they were always waiting for opportunities to show their worth, and to prove that they ought to have been chosen. Not surprisingly this led to fights breaking out between members of the rival groups whenever they met in the city. There are cities today, of course, where rival street gangs fight like this, but the extraordinary thing about Sparta was that there this sort of behaviour was promoted and controlled by the city itself.

Conclusion

To us the Spartan system of education hardly seems to be education at all. We should call it a harsh training designed to produce warriors, and that of course is what it was. But the Spartans thought that this was an adequate education because their whole way of life was so different from ours. We might think of an educated person as someone who has read a lot, knows a lot and, most important of all, can think for himself. But the Spartans did not want citizens who thought for themselves and had their own ideas. When a Spartan child was asked a question like 'Was Leonidas a brave hero?', he was not expected to think about it, consider the good and bad things about Leonidas and then give his own honest opinion. He was expected to answer, 'Yes. Leonidas was a brave hero,' because Leonidas was accepted as a brave hero by the city. The Spartan child was expected to learn the traditional answers to all questions and not to form his own personal view of any matter. He was also encouraged to give his answers, and indeed to conduct all conversation, in as few words and as clearly as possible. We still use the word 'laconic' to describe a style that is terse and to the point. The Spartans disliked long and complicated argument for the same reason that they did not want children to have their own opinions about things: they disliked and distrusted anything that interfered with the simple view of life that they had adopted.

The Spartans thought of an educated man as one who was devoted to the city and his fellow citizens, reliable in peace and war, courageous, obedient and well behaved according to their standards. These were the qualities they admired in a man, and these were the qualities their education was designed to produce.

CHAPTER SIX

Social Life

If we ask, 'What did the Spartan men do in their spare time?' or 'What sort of private lives did they lead?', the answer is very simple. They did not have any spare time or private life to speak of. As one ancient historian said, 'No Spartan was allowed to live just as he pleased. The whole city was a sort of camp in which every man had his ration of food allotted to him and what he was to do laid down for him.' The Spartan Equals divided almost all their time between military training and life in the barracks. That was the price they chose to pay to remain an elite of warriors supported by slave labour. In this chapter we shall look at the only three things that really broke the routine of the military way of life, and at the position of women.

Festivals

All Greek cities held festivals in honour of their favourite gods and goddesses. Besides being religious celebrations these festivals, which sometimes lasted several days, were the only holidays the Greeks had. (They did not have weeks or week-ends.) Unfortunately we do not know how many festivals Sparta had, although we know that she had fewer than Athens, but it is safe to guess that at the very least thirty days or so were devoted to festivals each year.

These festivals were generally celebrated with dancing and singing competitions. The competitions were between teams or choirs, of course, and not between individuals, and women and children took part in them as well as men.

There was one kind of religious occasion that the Spartans, unlike other Greeks, did not like to celebrate too extensively, and that was the funeral ceremony. In Athens, funeral ceremonies were accompanied by long periods of mourning and various superstitions about death were firmly believed. Athenian dead were buried with coins in their mouths and flasks of drink and food. The coins were to pay the ferryman Charon who was believed to take the dead across the underground river Styx to the Underworld. The food and drink were for the dead to take on the journey.

The Spartans, however, tried to minimise fear of death, naturally enough, since they were a race of soldiers. The time allowed for mourning was therefore limited by law, and no money, food or drink was put in the graves. The dead were buried within the city boundaries so that everybody, especially children, would become used to the sight of corpses and would not have superstitious fears about walking over graves.

Hunting

Hunting was one of the few activities that were regarded as a sport or relaxation at Sparta, although this too had a practical purpose, for it was one important way of obtaining food. The Spartans hunted on foot and with hounds; their hounds were famous throughout Greece for their keen scent. But even their customs when hunting show how the Spartans organised every aspect of their life with a view to the community rather than the individual. For instance, it was established practice for a party of men out hunting to seal up in jars any food they had left over after a meal, and to leave it in some obvious, but protected, spot for other parties of hunters who might pass that way. It was also an accepted custom that any Spartan might make use of any *helot* if he had need of him, no matter whose estate the *helot* technically belonged to, and this habit of borrowing applied also to hunting-hounds, and horses. A Spartan far from the city would simply borrow a horse from an outlying estate if he needed to, without feeling that it was necessary to ask permission. Naturally he treated the animal with care and had it returned after he had finished with it, otherwise this system of easy borrowing would soon have broken down.

Marriage

A Spartan Equal was not allowed to marry until the age of thirty, when he might leave his barracks. The women could be younger. After the wedding – we know nothing about the ceremony – the bride had her hair cut short like a boy's, and she was dressed in a man's cloak and sandals. At first her husband would visit her only at night.

The point of these customs is not altogether clear, but it seems possible that the man's clothes were supposed to show that the woman had submitted to the control of her husband, and the secret visits and lack of real meeting between husband and wife indicate that the marriage was only a trial one to begin with. This is likely to be at least part of the explanation, since the whole question of children was obviously very important to the Spartans. They were

29 *A hunting scene.*　　　　30 *Huntsman and dog.*

a few trying to rule over many. It was vital to them that marriages should produce children. For the same reason they adopted an even stranger custom from our point of view: if a couple had no children it was considered quite proper for a man to invite a younger man to sleep with his wife, in the hope that this union would produce a child.

So important were children to the state that various penalties were attached to bachelorhood. But it was not enough that there should be children; there had to be healthy children. As soon as a baby was born, instead of being washed in water, it was washed in wine. The Spartans did this because they believed – quite wrongly, of course – that a weak or sick child would simply die if washed in wine, whereas a strong child would somehow be strengthened still more. But that was not all: a child who survived the wine test still had to be accepted by the city. The father had to take his child before certain elders whose job it was to decide whether the baby was likely to grow up strong or weak. A simple society like Sparta, without much medical knowledge or skill, could do little to help someone who was crippled, and the unfortunate person would be unable to help the Equals maintain their warrior way of life. If the elders decided that a baby looked strong enough, they declared that it could be brought up as a citizen, and it was at this point that an estate was granted to the future warrior. But if they felt that the baby was too weak, or deformed in some way, they ordered that it should be left to die in a chasm by a near-by mountain.

Spartan women

Spartan girls (that is, the daughters of the Equals) were not brought up to perform such tasks as weaving and spinning, as girls in other cities were. In Sparta such activities were fit only for slaves. Instead, the girls did a certain amount of physical training with the boys (they wore special tunics with a slit at the side to enable them to move easily), and, presumably, since we know they took part in various dancing and singing competitions, they also joined the boys in learning to play the lyre, to dance, and to recite or chant poetry. They did not, however, join in the military training. And they did not live in barracks, but at home.

What were they being brought up to do? Sparta was organised in such a way that everybody from *helot* to Equal had a particular function, a specific job to do. What were women to do in Sparta? The job of women in most societies has traditionally been very much centred on the family, but in Sparta, with the boys and men away at the barracks, there really was no such thing as a family. There was not even any shopping for the women to do, since all food was provided by the *helots*. It may seem that Sparta must have been the sort of place that members of Women's Liberation movements today would have admired: a place in which women were freed from

31 *Bronze statuette of a Spartan girl running.*

domestic duties and treated like men. But this was not the case. Women had their special job to do just like everybody else in Sparta, and it was to produce healthy children. That was why they exercised with the boys; the object was to make them strong and healthy so that their children would be strong and healthy too. And for the same reason Spartan women continued training through the early months of pregnancy and ate and drank freely, whereas in other Greek cities

32 *A painting by Degas of Spartan boys and girls exercising.*

mothers lived quietly at home before their children were born, and were careful to eat and drink sparingly. Apparently these measures worked, for the Spartans were remarkable for their size and strength. A foreigner once asked the wife of King Leonidas why Spartan women were able to influence men more than wives in other cities. 'We are the only women who can control men,' she replied, 'because we are the only women who give birth to men.'

The pride of a Spartan woman, then, was to be the mother of a truly courageous member of the Equals. There are stories of mothers who carried this so far that they would much prefer their children to be killed honourably in battle than to survive without honour. For instance, one mother, seeing her son returning after a battle, asked him how the city had fared. 'All have perished,' he replied. His mother picked up a tile and hurled it at him, shouting, 'And so they sent you to bring us the bad news.' The tile killed him. This attitude, of course, was quite in keeping with the spirit of Tyrtaeus' poetry and with the spirit of Sparta in general. To die for the city:

that was man's highest honour. And that was what a mother dreamed of for her sons.

The reputation of Spartan women

What Spartan women were really like is a bit of a mystery: so many contradictory things were said about them. Despite the fact that Athenian comic writers made fun of them as beefy, masculine creatures, they had a reputation for great beauty. If they deserved this reputation, they must have had a natural beauty, since jewellery and ornaments were frowned upon.

They certainly had more freedom than other Greek women. Athenian women, for instance, stayed very much at home, occupying themselves with household tasks and obeying their husbands in all matters. But since Spartan women did not really have a family to look after, it seems quite likely that they may have been rather bored.

33 *An ivory comb from Sparta depicting the judgement of Paris. Seventh century* BC.

This may explain why they earned a reputation for being rather unruly and sexually promiscuous (although this reputation may have arisen as a result of other Greeks being mystified by the strange marriage customs of the Spartans).

Women and land

One rather odd thing is certain. This city, which was planned as a society for male warriors, gradually became dominated by women.

In addition to their relative freedom, the Spartan women gradually gained control of much of the city's private estates, and thereby acquired great power and influence. How they gained control of the land is not exactly clear, but it may have been due to the fact that the Equals were not allowed to own more than the city had originally granted them, and when the number of Equals was reduced by war the vacant estates may have been taken over by the women. At any rate, not long after the period of Sparta's history that concerns us (700–400 BC), Sparta was dominated by a number of very wealthy women. But by that time the whole system at Sparta had broken down.

CHAPTER SEVEN

Spartan Government

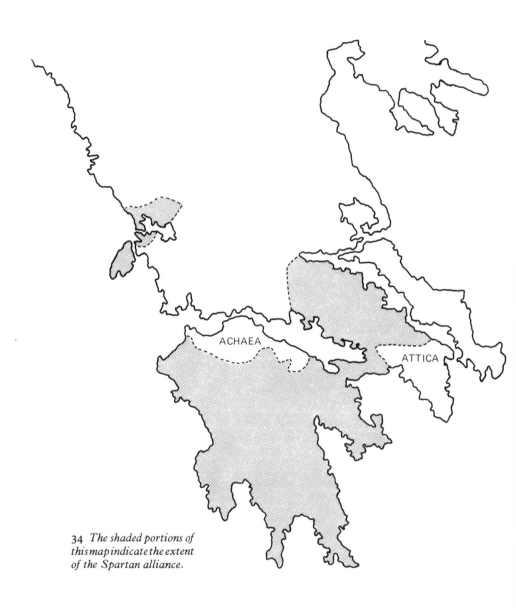

34 *The shaded portions of
this map indicate the extent
of the Spartan alliance.*

ACHAEA

ATTICA

Besides ruling over a large area of land and a great number of people, the Spartans were also for a long time at the head of a league of allied cities (the Peloponnesian League), and many people turned to them at one time or another for help or protection. How did Sparta organise her own government? Who made decisions about whether to answer a request for help, about what went on in the city itself or about what was to be done about an attempted uprising of the *helots*? The Spartans ruled Laconia and Messenia, but who ruled the Spartans? The answer is that whereas other cities had, or had had at one time, either kings or a council of a few citizens, or a democratic assembly of all the citizens to govern them, Sparta had a little bit of everything. Her government consisted of kings, council, five magistrates known as *ephors*, and an Assembly of all the Equals. (Women at Sparta, like women in all Greek cities, had no official political power at all.)

Kings

There were two royal families in Sparta. When either of the kings died, he was succeeded by the eldest surviving son of those children who had been born during his reign. A son who had been born before his father had actually become king could not succeed to the throne. If the heir was not old enough to rule, he was none the less accepted as king, but a close relative ruled as regent in his place.

The powers of the kings

Sparta retained her kings, although all other Greek cities had got rid of theirs at an early date in their history, but she left them with limited powers. Spartan kings did not resemble the early kings of England, who were entitled to do more or less as they pleased. They were much more like our present Queen in that their power, like hers, was in practice very restricted, although they still had much of the honour and dignity traditionally associated with royalty.

In the city itself, the kings had some of the duties of priests and slight authority as judges in certain specific cases, and that was all. They were responsible for making sacrifices to the gods and for leading the citizens in their religious celebrations; and they conducted legal cases involving the adoption of children and the marrying of wealthy orphan girls.

Their only real power was as commanders in battle. In theory, they had the right to declare war without reference to anybody else, but in fact they never did act alone in this way. Once on the battlefield, however, they were supreme. Originally, in time of war both kings had led the Equals out together. This practice was stopped after two kings quarrelled while on campaign: one withdrew his troops, thus ruining the success of the expedition. After that, a law was passed forbidding both kings to be away from the city on a campaign at the same time.

As well as having only limited power, the kings could also be punished for misconduct, or even deposed. If a battle was a failure, the king in command might be fined. And if things in general were going badly for the city, the kings might be held responsible, since they, as the city's priests, were the people who were supposed to keep the gods favourable.

Yet they were normally held in considerable honour. They were extremely rich (technically much of the land worked by the *perioeci* belonged to the royal families); they were served double rations of food in their *syssitia*, they had seats of honour at festivals, and the whole Assembly of Equals stood up when the kings arrived. Surprisingly, in view of the fact that funerals at Sparta were not allowed to be extravagant, the kings were never more conspicuously honoured than at their death, as the following passage shows:

Horsemen carried the news of the death of a king throughout the whole territory of Sparta, and women moved through the city itself, beating cauldrons in lamentation. On this signal one man and one woman in each household had to put on mourning clothes or else they were heavily fined. Many thousands of people – Spartans, *perioeci* and *helots* – were obliged by law to attend the funeral. They beat their foreheads as a sign of grief, wailing and moaning, and cried out that the dead king was the best king that they had ever had. (Plutarch, *Life of Lycurgus*.)

The Gerousia

The kings were also automatically members of the Council of Elders or *Gerousia*. There were twenty-eight other members, making thirty in all. The main task of this council was to prepare proposals which could then be brought before the full Assembly of Equals for their vote; but it also acted as a court for trying criminal cases, such as those involving charges of murder and treason, and it could impose punishments, including the death sentence, and decrees dishonouring an individual.

To be a member of the *Gerousia* one had to be an Equal over the age of sixty. The election worked as follows: a number of people who were to act as judges in the election shut themselves up in a house. All the Equals then assembled near the house and the candidates for election to the *Gerousia* were brought forward one at a time. Those people who wanted to support a particular candidate simply shouted as loudly as they could. The judges in the near-by house calculated the volume of applause that was given to each candidate and announced as winners those who seemed to them to have received the most.

The philosopher Aristotle, who was something of an expert in political affairs, understandably thought that this was a very silly way of electing people to an important office. He had other criticisms to make, too. 'It would be all right,' he wrote, 'if the people elected could be counted on to behave wisely and virtuously. But as a matter of fact they can't be. There is evidence that members of the *Gerousia* have been guilty of bribery and favouritism. Besides, people's minds grow old, as well as their bodies.' Aristotle was very doubtful about the wisdom of a council of men over the age of sixty, since once a man was elected, he remained a councillor for life, regardless of how old he became and how much his mind began to wander. 'It would be better,' Aristotle concluded, 'if the council's meetings could be observed by the people and if in some way it could be made answerable for its decisions, neither of which is the case.'

The ephorate

The *ephorate* is both the most interesting and the most obscure of offices under the Spartan constitution. It seems that the *ephors* became more important and gained in political power as the history of Sparta proceeded. Originally, the *ephorate* may have consisted simply of officials appointed by the kings to help them carry out their many duties. But, as we have already seen, by the time with which we are concerned the kings had lost a lot of their power, and it is certain that the *ephors* had gained a great deal of what the kings had lost.

There were five *ephors*, elected each year by the full Assembly of Equals. Anybody who was a Spartan Equal and over thirty years old was allowed to stand for election. The responsibilities of the *ephors* included giving foreign ambassadors permission to cross the border into Spartan territory and permission to address the Assembly.

But the main duties of the *ephors* were what we should call executive duties; that is to say, they were responsible in various ways for seeing that the state functioned smoothly, that the laws were upheld and that nobody exerted more than his rightful power. For instance, once the state had decided by vote of the Assembly to go to war, it was the *ephors* who were responsible for calling out the army and deciding precisely how many troops should be sent out. They also had the power to direct generals to particular campaigns, and when one of the kings was acting as commander in the field he was always accompanied by two of the *ephors*.

In addition, the *ephors* had absolute power over all the other magistrates. They controlled the *Crypteia* and the state finances; and they had overall responsibility for the education of the Spartan young and the maintenance of discipline throughout the community. They could fine people on the spot (once they fined a man for being lazy and another man for being unpopular!); and as well as joining with the *Gerousia* in conducting criminal trials, they also had sole responsibility for conducting trials involving civil offences. Finally, they had the job of summoning meetings of the *Gerousia* and the Assembly.

35 *Spartan warriors relaxing.*

The Assembly

The *ephors*, therefore, undoubtedly had great power. But it was limited in an important way by the fact that the Assembly elected the *ephors*. The Assembly consisted of all full Spartans (Equals) over the age of thirty and it met outside the city under the shelter of a huge canopy – a tent without sides.

Questions of peace and war and foreign policy had to be decided by a vote of the Assembly, as did the appointment of generals and any proposed changes in the law. But despite the fact that the Assembly was therefore responsible for some important decisions, it seems that it was not able to put forward its own proposals; they had to come from the *Gerousia*. Nor was the Assembly able to debate issues. Instead, it listened to the debating between kings, *ephors* and councillors, and then simply voted for or against a proposal. But its vote carried the day even against a proposal put forward unanimously by the councillors.

How Spartan government worked in practice

In practice it is fairly clear that the *ephorate* had the political power and influence in time of peace, and the kings had the authority in war. Nevertheless, we must remember that it was the Assembly that had the final say on a proposal, and elected the members of the *Gerousia* and the *ephors*, and it was from members of the Assembly that the *ephors* were elected each year.

The way the system worked is clear from what happened before the outbreak of the Peloponnesian war against Athens and her allies. Various council members no doubt spoke; amongst them was King Archidamus, who advised the Spartans to reject the proposal that they should declare war at that moment, and the *ephor* Sthenelaides, who gave the opposite advice. But it was the Assembly of Equals that finally made the decision. The decision was to go to war.

EPILOGUE

We said in the Introduction that there has never been a state quite like the city state of Sparta. There never has been – quite. And perhaps for most of us, brought up in a very different kind of community, this is just as well. It is understandable that most historians should feel that Sparta was a most unpleasant place.

Nevertheless a number of people, such as the Athenian philosopher Plato, have greatly admired Sparta. What they admired has really been three aspects of the Spartan way of life. First, the idea of an equal community in which all citizens share things amongst themselves and co-operate, rather than compete, with each other. (Although it must not be forgotten that the Spartans only managed to live in this way by using the slave labour of the *helots*.) Secondly, the discipline and order of the Spartan system. Nothing was left to chance; none of the Equals was left alone to rely on luck. Provided that a man did his duty, he could rely on the others to stand by him. The state provided security. Thirdly, without necessarily admiring what the Spartans regarded as their duty, many people have been impressed by the notion of a city in which all the citizens have a strong sense of loyalty and duty to each other and to the life of the community.

Comparisons with Sparta

There are also a number of countries that may be compared in some ways with Sparta. Generally there is not much resemblance between the whole way of life of Sparta and other countries, but rather between particular areas of life. For instance the intense patriotism of the Spartans and their willingness, almost eagerness, to die for their country, has been matched many times. It might be compared in particular with the patriotism of certain Japanese suicide pilots in the Second World War. Such was their loyalty to Japan, in the person of the Emperor, that they were willing to fly their planes deliberately into a target – a ship, for instance. This guaranteed an explosion and the destruction of the target. It also guaranteed the death of the pilot. Again, there are similarities between the way in which Spartan youths were trained and the kind of training the United States gives to its crack fighting force, the marines. The American marines of course have what we regard as a normal education in school. But once they enlist as marines they are trained as ruthlessly as any Spartan ever was, and are turned into fighting men with the same kind of courage and strength.

To take an example from our own country, the public school tradition of education, although it differed in certain important respects from the Spartan system, was modelled closely on Sparta in some ways. The boarding system, the emphasis on sport, the system of prefects, and above all the emphasis on what is sometimes called 'the stiff upper lip' and teaching the child to stand on his own two feet the hard way, were all a conscious imitation of the Spartan ideal.

Many similarities may also be observed between Sparta and Russia. There are of course many important differences between the two, and it would be quite wrong to judge Russia by reference to Sparta. But there are many points of comparison. The communist system resembles the way in which the Equals shared land and wealth. The Russian political system, which attempts to combine rule by all the people with government by the party leaders, is not dissimilar to the Spartan attempt to combine the power of the Assembly with the power of the *ephors*. There is a similarity between the Russian distrust of composers and writers whose work does not reflect the accepted attitudes of the state, and the Spartan distrust of new values and change in art. Above all there is a close resemblance between the Russian and the Spartan demand for unquestioning loyalty to the state. But perhaps the most striking analogy of all with Sparta is provided by the police state of South Africa, where the policy of apartheid seems uncomfortably similar to the Spartans' attitude towards the *helots*.

Sparta during the Persian wars

As we have seen, the Equals were not trained to conquer the world so much as to keep the *helots* in their place. The Spartans were a race of warriors, but we must not picture them as a horde of swashbuckling conquering heroes. They were a people who suddenly and dramatically decided to turn their backs on all the usual pleasures of life, in order to be able to survive as masters of the huge *helot* population. The city became a disciplined and efficient machine, and the Spartans' prime consideration was to ensure that the machine functioned smoothly. Their interest was a secure and stable life. They were content to leave others to themselves, and, originally at least, they had no great plans for conquest or empire, provided that nobody troubled them. And nobody did. Foreign armies did not choose to invade Laconia and take on the Spartan machine.

Sparta's policy of keeping herself to herself at times amounted to little more than selfishness. At the beginning of the fifth century, when Persia invaded Greece, Sparta was slow to consider the common interest of the Greeks.

The Persians first landed at Marathon in Attica (490 BC). The Athenians sent a runner with an urgent message for help to Sparta. (The runner ran for three days without stopping; hence our phrase 'marathon runner', meaning a long-distance runner.) But the Spartans replied that they could not come at once, as they were in the middle of a religious festival. This was possibly a reasonable excuse by Greek standards, in view of the importance attached to the gods and their worship. But the Athenians may well have felt resentful and suspicious when the Spartans finally appeared on the hill over-looking the plain of Marathon after the battle was over.

Ten years later they again had good reason to suspect the Spartans of selfishness. On this occasion, when the Persians were invading for the second time, the Spartans tried to insist that the Greeks should set up their defences at the narrow entry to the Peloponnese on the isthmus of Corinth. This may have been a good position to defend, but it meant handing Athens over to the enemy without a fight. It was only with great difficulty and a certain amount of cunning that the Athenian commander, Themistocles, managed to press the Spartans into abandoning this proposal. (However, we must not forget that this was just after Leonidas and the 300 Spartans defended Thermopylae.)

Sparta and the Peloponnesian war

Once the Persian wars were over, Sparta retired again into her own territory, while Athens rapidly developed a wealthy and powerful empire. Sparta did very little to interfere, until at last the states that, for one reason or another, resented the growing strength of Athens began to urge her to lead some resistance. Even then it took some time and effort to get the Spartans to go to war. This was the occasion when King Archidamus argued in favour of caution and delay, but the Assembly of Equals finally chose to follow the advice of the *ephor* Sthenelaidas. Before the final decision, the Corinthian ambassadors told the Spartans in no uncertain terms that they were blind to the real threat of the Athenian empire: 'You Spartans are the only Greeks who wait calmly until things have actually happened. You wait until the enemy has doubled his strength before you act. We don't dispute that you have a great reputation for strength and courage,' they added, but they suggested that it was sometimes difficult to see how Sparta had earned this reputation, since she was always so slow to act. The Corinthians went on to point out that the

Spartans seemed quite unaware that the Athenians could not be judged as if they were Spartans. The Spartans were making a great mistake if they assumed that the Athenians were as uninterested in extending their power as they themselves were. The Spartans and the Athenians were as different as chalk and cheese, as the Corinthians put it:

The Athenians are sharp fellows, full of bright ideas, quick to think of something and quick to carry it out. You Spartans are good at keeping things as they are. You never produce original ideas. You seldom bother to achieve all that you could. You hang back and concentrate on your own country alone – but the Athenians are for ever expanding their control and influence abroad.

The Peloponnesian war lasted, on and off, for thirty years. Finally it was Sparta and her allies who were victorious. The Athenians were defeated; their empire was broken up, their power and wealth taken away; and for a while even their famous democracy came to

36 *The shaded portions of this map indicate the extent of the Athenian empire.*

EUBOEA

LYDIA

CRETE

an end. The Spartan conquerors destroyed the Athenian defensive walls and left the city with only ten ships and a government of thirty pro-Spartan dictators. But this victory was also the beginning of the end for Sparta.

The weakness in the Spartan system

Sparta had won the war, but only just. The number of Equals was now very low, and there must have been some who wondered whether sacrificing everything to produce a warrior class made much sense, when those warriors had such difficulty in defeating a non-professional enemy. But the real trouble was yet to come. Sparta had brought her citizens up to understand only one way of life, but now a new way of life was being presented to them.

Sparta had power and influence abroad, and naturally enough she began to build up her own empire in place of the Athenian one, sending commanders out to control garrisons in various cities. This meant that her commanders were surrounded by wealth and luxuries they had never experienced before. They were not able to resist

temptation. Men like Lysander began to glory in fine clothes, rich food and expensive jewellery. Away from the strict control of Sparta, power went to Lysander's head. He became proud and arrogant. Soon allies refused to serve under him. He was recalled, and then it was discovered that he was smuggling riches into Sparta itself. The same sort of thing happened in many cases. Despite their strict education and upbringing, the Spartans who were away from home could not resist luxury and wealth, when there was an opportunity to acquire them. Before the war, Archidamus had urged the Spartans never to lose hold of the discipline that had been handed down by their fathers. But now the discipline was going.

37 *A Spartan warrior.*

The battle of Leuctra

The final blow came in 371 BC. A Spartan army was routed at Leuctra by the Thebans, and following this the Thebans, under Epaminondas, marched rapidly down into the Peloponnese, right to the city of Sparta itself. It was the first time that a foreign army had dared to invade Laconia. The shock must have been tremendous, and the Spartans never really recovered. Too much had gone wrong: the myth that her warriors were unbeatable was quite shattered; the number of Equals was down to less than a thousand; her famous discipline was no longer effective; corruption had led to great inequalities of wealth even amongst the Equals (much of the wealth being in the hands of women). Sparta no longer resembled the city she had once been.

Perhaps the last time the Spartans really showed the spirit for which they were famous was just before the Theban invasion, when the news of the defeat at Leuctra arrived at the city:

The Spartans happened to be celebrating a solemn festival and the boys were dancing in the theatre, when the message containing news of the defeat at Leuctra arrived. The *ephors* realised that the blow was fatal to Sparta and that her power would never be the same again. But they gave orders that the festival should continue and that the dancing should not be stopped. Meanwhile each family which had lost a relative in the battle was informed privately. On the next day all those whose relatives had been killed in the battle came into the market-place with proud smiles. It was the families of the survivors who stayed at home in shame. (Plutarch, *Life of Lycurgus*.)

To die fighting for his city – what could be more glorious than this for a Spartan?

Date (BC)	Greece	Sparta
1150–	Dorians invade Greece.	Most settle in Peloponnese.
900–		Spartans gain control of Laconia.
800–	Kings replaced by aristocracies in most Greek cities.	Kings retained.
700–	Trade and colonisation under way. Tyrants take over in some Greek cities.	c. 736–716 1st Messenian war. c. 650–630 2nd Messenian war. c. 620 changes at Sparta (attributed to Lycurgus).
600– 500	Gradual emergence of demo-cracy at Athens, culminating in Cleisthenes' reforms in 508 BC.	Sparta isolates herself, and perfects her new way of life.
490	1st Persian invasion. Battle of Marathon.	Spartans arrive too late at Marathon.
480	2nd Persian invasion (under Xerxes). Battles of Thermopylae, Salamis and Plataea (479).	Leonidas and the Three Hundred defend Thermopylae.
478	Athenians form Delian League with Ionian allies. During the next 20 years the League gradually turns into an empire controlled by Athens.	
464 (?)	Athenians send help to the Spartans against the helots. The help is rejected.	A serious uprising by the helots who defend themselves on Mount Ithome.
462– 445	Very uneasy relations between Athens and Sparta. During these years Athens becomes more democratic under the guidance of Pericles.	
445 431	A thirty-year peace treaty made between Athens and Sparta. The peace comes to an end. The Peloponnesian war between Athens and Sparta and their allies begins. It will last, with intervals, until 404.	
429	Death of Pericles.	
424		Serious loss for Sparta at Pylos, where many of the Equals are captured.
421	Peace of Nicias between Athens and Sparta.	
415	The Athenians launch an enormous invasion of Sicily, which ends in disaster (413).	Despite the peace, skirmishing continues between the two sides.

Date (BC)	Greece	Sparta
411	Athenian democracy suspended for a short time, following the troubles the Athenians face after their defeat in Sicily.	
404	The war ends with the defeat of Athens by Sparta.	
403		Sparta begins to set up pro-Spartan governments in other cities and to send out governors. Many of the governors become corrupted by power and wealth.
402		Lysander is deposed.
395–389	Athens, Thebes, Corinth and Argos join together to challenge Spartan supremacy. Athenians form another league of allies.	
389–380		Sparta regains some of her power.
371	The Peace of Callias. Peace is made between all the warring states of Greece. But Sparta and Thebes quarrel over some of the terms.	
371		Spartans defeated by the Thebans at the battle of Leuctra. Epaminondas, the Theban general, marches on Sparta itself.

FURTHER STUDY

A Reading
B Follow-up Work

FURTHER STUDY A

Reading

The teacher may find H. Michell's *Sparta* (Cambridge University Press 1952) useful for further information on social aspects of Sparta, and W. G. Forrest's *A History of Sparta 950-192 BC* (Hutchinson 1968) useful for further information on historical aspects. V. Ehrenberg's *From Solon to Socrates* (Methuen 1968) provides a scholarly history of the main part of the period covered in this book. A. R. Burn's *Pelican History of Greece* (Pelican 1966) provides a more readable history of Greece, from its prehistorical beginnings down to its conquest by Rome. Unfortunately, neither Plutarch's *Life of Lycurgus* nor Xenophon's *Constitution of the Lacedaimonians*, which despite their inadequacy remain our main sources for Sparta, is readily available in cheap editions. Both are obtainable in translation, however, in the Loeb series, published by Heinemann. Both Plutarch and Xenophon, if available, may well be read by the student, as may the remaining books mentioned here.

Mary Renault's *The Last of the Wine* (Longmans 1956) is a novel set against the background of the Peloponnesian war. George Orwell's *1984*, his *Animal Farm*, and Aldous Huxley's *Brave New World* (all Penguin Books) may also be of interest as modern pictures of totalitarian states.

Certain aspects of the Spartan way of life, mentioned in this book, may be looked at in more depth, in the wider context of the Greek and Roman world, in the other books in this series.

FURTHER STUDY B

Follow-up Work

1. Finding out about the Spartans is not easy, because they themselves did not write anything down. They did not write about their way of life or their history. They did not even write plays, as the Athenians did, from which one can learn a certain amount about the sort of things that interest a people and what their attitudes are to various problems. (The theatre at Sparta was a place for recitations and

musical competitions, not a place for putting on plays.) To see how plays and stories can indirectly tell us about a people or society, choose a television play or serial – it does not matter if it is fictional – watch it carefully, and then try to list all the things you have discovered from it about the way of life of the characters.

2. Most of the information about the Spartans in this book comes from two essays by Plutarch and Xenophon. Both were Greeks, but neither was Spartan. Xenophon lived during the fifth century, but he was an Athenian, and although he was an admirer of Sparta, he may not have known as much about the Spartans as he would have us believe. Plutarch lived several centuries after the period about which he was writing. Neither writer, then, is entirely reliable. You can see for yourself how cautious one needs to be in relying on second-hand reports by getting hold of several newspapers and seeing the different way in which each treats the same story. Make lists of the different items of factual information the various papers give and the different comments they make on the facts.

3. Quite often during the course of this book I have compared Sparta with Athens. This is partly because Athens was one of the great Greek city states, and partly because we know more about Athens than about any other city. Find out more about Athens from books in your school or public library.

4. *The Battle of Thermopylae*
   (a) Read the description of this battle and the events leading up to it given by the historian Herodotus in his *Histories* (Penguin), Book 7, especially pp. 487 ff.
   (b) Draw a picture of Leonidas and the three hundred Spartans at Thermopylae, either just before the battle or during it.
   (c) Do you think that Leonidas and his men showed true courage, or were they unnecessarily reckless in throwing away their lives (or a bit of both)? Either write your views down or have a class discussion.
   (d) Write a short play, set in Sparta, about a family, one of whom is away at Thermopylae. Try to include scenes that take place before it is known that the Persians have found a way to get round the Greeks and after the news of the death of the three hundred has reached Sparta.

5. *Pylos*
   (a) Read Thucydides' account of the events leading up to this defeat for Sparta in his *History of the Peloponnesian War* (Penguin), pp. 230–54.
   (b) Write an imaginary newspaper report of the capture of the Spartans as it might have been written in Sparta.
   (c) Write a short account of the sort of conversation you imagine the Spartans on Sphacteria might have had just before they were captured.

6. *The debate at Sparta before the outbreak of the Peloponnesian war*

(a) Read Thucydides' account of this debate in his history of the war (pp. 77–81).

(b) Write a conversation that might have taken place between the members of a *syssition* after the debate.

7. *Leuctra*

Try to imagine the thoughts and feelings the mother of a Spartan warrior killed at Leuctra might have experienced, then write a short passage describing them.

8. *Syssitia*

(a) Draw a picture of the members of a *syssition* dining together.

(b) Imagine that the day has come for you to try to win election to a *syssition*. Describe your feelings before and after election.

9. *Perioeci*

If you had been one of the *perioeci* would you have been content or would you have wanted to rebel against the Spartans? Either write down your views or have a class discussion.

10. *Helots*

(a) Why did the Spartans treat the *helots* in the way they did?

(b) If you had to be one or the other, would you rather have been a Spartan *helot* or an Athenian slave? (Find out about Athenian slaves from Kenneth Hughes' *Slavery*, in this series.)

11. *Exposure*

The Spartans were not the only Greeks who exposed young children to die if they were weak or unwanted. It was common practice amongst all the Greeks.

(a) One of the most famous of Athenian plays, Sophocles' *Oedipus Rex* (Penguin), tells how Oedipus' parents, frightened by an oracle which says that their son will grow up to kill his father and marry his mother, give the baby to a slave to abandon on the mountainside. But the slave does not do so. Find out what happens by reading the play or consulting a good encyclopedia.

(b) What differences in life today make the exposure of children unnecessary and unacceptable?

12. *Athletics, Sports and Games*

(a) Find out more about athletics in the ancient world from John Murrell's *Athletics, Sports and Games* (in this series).

(b) Are the games you play, both at school and at home, mainly team games or not? What do you think are the advantages and disadvantages of team games?

13. *Education*

Describe a day 'at school' for a Spartan boy of your age, and then describe your day at your school, bringing out the differences between the two. Say at the end which kind of education you prefer and why. You might like to have a class debate about this.

14. *Women*

(a) What do you think of the sort of education a Spartan girl received?

(b) Women in most Greek states stayed very much at home and were expected to obey their husbands. As we have seen, they had no political rights anywhere. There is an amusing comedy by the Athenian Aristophanes, *Lysistrata*, in which the story hinges upon a decision by the women to force their husbands to stop the Peloponnesian war. One of the characters is a Spartan girl named Lampito. She is pictured as tough and athletic.

(c) Describe a day in the life of a Spartan woman, bringing out the advantages and disadvantages of the sort of life Spartan women led.

15. *Government*

(a) Do you agree with Aristotle that, in some ways at least, the Spartan system of government was silly?

(b) How much power would the Assembly have had? Try to arrive at an answer to this question by going through the process of setting up a Spartan government in your class. First elect a few people to be councillors in the Spartan manner, and then let the council debate any point of interest, allowing the rest of the class to say only 'yes' or 'no' to proposals. Do the rest of the class feel that they have had much effect on what is finally decided?

16. Can you think of any songs, poems or hymns that represent for us something similar to what Tyrtaeus' poetry represented for the Spartans?

17. Find out what you can about Russia, China or South Africa today. Do you think these countries are really similar to Sparta? What do you think of them? Are they the sort of places where you would want to live?

18. Imagine that a time machine could transport you back to Sparta and that you are spending the day with a Spartan boy of your own age. What kind of criticism of his way of life would you make? What would you expect his reactions to be?

19. What would it have been like to be a Spartan? Taking everything into consideration, what is there to be said in favour of it and what is there to be said against it? Can you imagine enjoying or taking pride in being a Spartan? Organise a debate on the subject.

20. (a) Draw a picture of a meeting of the Spartan Assembly.

(b) Draw a picture of the funeral of a Spartan king.

(c) In English we still use the word 'spartan' as an adjective. What do you think it means? Check your answer in a dictionary.